THE WALKS

The River Dove tumbles beneath the limestone crags of Wolfscote Dale where, once, wild wolves could be found.

The walks included in this book have been devised with inexperienced walkers and family outings in mind. Whether or not you are experienced, however, you should never set out hill-walking without care or thought. You need to plan your day in advance. First read the walk account and become familiar with the route on good maps. Next, work out a rough schedule of walking, visits, rests and refreshments bearing in mind opening times. Equip yourself with the right kind of clothing and supplies.

Out on the ramble, keep your wits about you: field boundaries may have been moved, trees taken away, or new roads constructed. To give you some idea of what to expect, the walks have been graded. **Easy** walks take about two hours and are generally well signposted along made-up paths and tracks. **Moderate** walks take up to four hours or so; the terrain is mostly firm but there may be an occasional steep climb or rough track. **Difficult** walks need careful planning, take the best part of a day, and demand detailed maps, compass, refreshments, and suitable clothing. On long walks habitations are few, shelter is sparse, and the weather can about-turn in minutes. Yet walking in this wild landscape gives tremendous feelings of exhilaration. Whatever your interests there is a walk for you — so put one foot in front of the other, and repeat as necessary!

Countryside Care

The countryside lives and breathes. It is home for many, provides a living for some, and plays a vital role in our economy. It is also the basis of our natural heritage.

Those who walk in the countryside tread a tightrope: between access and conservation, involvement and interference, utilization and preservation. Organizations, such as the National Trust or National Park authorities, are dedicated to preserving our heritage by ensuring access to certain areas while at the same time planning for the future. Walkers enjoy the highlights of the countryside at their leisure, but they owe it to themselves and to others to conserve these pleasures for the generations to come. We have rights, but we also have responsibilities.

Rights of Way and Access

Public footpaths, tracks, and bridleways are 'public property' in the same sense as a road or car park. They are not owned by the public, however; the landowner, while retaining rights of ownership, 'dedicates' a path or road to public use so that a right of way is established.

A scattering of trees along the valley side of Wolfscote Dale might hint of forest but the Royal Forest of the Peak was simply an area set aside for hunting.

A right of way means the public is permitted to cross land by the designated route, without straying from it or causing damage. If you leave the path you may be trespassing; if you leave litter, or damage fences or crops, you lay yourself open to legal action. A right of way remains as such until it is revoked ('extinguished') in law, by the local authority. It is irrelevant how often the route is used, or whether it is overgrown, or blocked by a locked gate or a heap of manure. In some cases, however, rights of way may be diverted to permit buildings, roadworks, or farming.

Footpaths and other public rights of way are indicated on the Ordnance Survey 1:50 000 (Landranger) series. In addition, public access is customary in common land because fencing it to keep people out is both legally complex and impractical.

Beware of the Bull

Complicated bye-laws govern the release of bulls into fields crossed by a right of way. It is best to assume that any bull is potentially dangerous and to take a detour or avoid it if possible.

What to wear

For all but the shortest routes, the walker should be properly clothed. Purpose-designed boots and a waterproof top are not only sensible for comfort and safety, they also help you enjoy to the full your day out. The first essential is some type of waterproof and windproof outer garment such as an anorak, cagoule, or coat, preferably with a hood. Modern lightweight, 'breathable' anoraks can be rolled and stowed away when not in use.

For warmth, the main requirement is several layers of insulating material such as woollen sweaters or thermofleece garments. These can be taken off as the weather improves, or added to if the wind strengthens. Wool 'breathes' to minimize sweating yet retains body heat effectively. A warm shirt is also recommended.

Do not wear denim jeans for walking. They are usually too restrictive and have poor insulating qualities, especially when wet. Walking trousers should be warm and comfortably loose to allow movement without chafing. On long walks, carry waterproof overtrousers.

Feet are the walker's best friends, so care for them. There are as many opinions about the best kind of footwear for walking as there are feet on the footpaths. Nowadays, there is a huge range of boots and walking shoes available and it is sensible to buy the best that you can afford. Good outdoor clothing suppliers can advise you or, better still, read the reviews in the outdoor magazines and then buy the boots that suit you best. Good ankle support is a must in rocky and difficult terrain. For short walks on easy ground a pair of tough, comfortable shoes may be adequate. Wellingtons may be suited to very wet ground but they quickly become uncomfortable and tend to rub up blisters. Whatever the footwear, thick woollen or loop-stitch socks are the sensible choice beneath; at a price, the so-called 'super-socks' are now available. Most footwear needs to be broken in and must fit comfortably before you take to the paths.

A small brook bubbles through an attractively wooded section of the Derwent Valley. The trees are showing the beginnings of their autumn colours.

The Peak National Park

During the 1930s, mill workers, who craved for the air and freedom of the open moors, were denied access to the privately owned grouse moors of the High Peak. Confrontations with gamekeepers occurred. Matters came to a head and, on 24 Aprii 1932, 600 ramblers set off on a mass trespass that resulted in jail sentences for some. The seeds of public access were sown, however, and, after World War 2, as part of the government's reconstruction plan, National Parks were established. The aim was to protect and to enhance the special qualities of landscape and to encourage suitable recreational activities.

The Peak National Park was the first to be designated in 1951. Over 500 square miles (1295 sq km) are encompassed within the Park boundary, with 76 square miles (197 sq km) of high moorland open to walkers by negotiated access agreements with the landowners.

A stone's throw from Sheffield and Chesterfield, Baslow Edge is popular with walkers.

On longer walks it is wise to carry a few extras in your rucksack: a sweater, a spare pair of socks, a warm hat, and a pair of thermal gloves.

What to take

Certain items are basic to any respectable walk. A rucksack and good maps are vital. Other equipment depends on the nature of the walk and personal interests. The rucksack or backpack has many advantages over a hand-carried bag. With a rucksack you can take more, carry it more comfortably, and leave your hands free (an important safety consideration in rough terrain). There is an enormous variety of rucksacks available. For a half-day or day walk choose a medium-sized model of about 30 litres capacity, made of nylon or similar, that fits you snugly without chafing.

A selection of maps should always be at hand. Do not rely solely on the sketch maps in this book. These sketch maps are intended for use with Ordnance Survey maps (1:50 000 Landranger series or, better, the Outdoor Leisure Maps and Pathfinder maps at 1:25 000 – about 2½ inches to the mile).

A good map provides details of rights of way, viewpoints, parking, conveniences, and telephones, and lets you identify distant features. A compass is necessary for map-reading because paths are often indistinct or routes unmarked across open country. Local guidebooks and field guides point out items of interest as you go, rather than after you return.

On a long walk, carry extra food with you unless you are sure of a 'refuelling' stop. Concentrated high-energy food, such as chocolate or mintcake, revives flagging limbs and spirits, and a modern lightweight vacuum-flask provides a welcome hot beverage. A few sticking plasters, a penknife, and a length of string may come in handy so keep them in a side pocket in your rucksack. A modern 'blister-repair kit' can be a real boon.

Walking is an excellent way of reaching an unusual viewpoint or approaching wary wildlife. A camera records the scene and 'collects' nature without damaging it, and binoculars permit close-ups of animals about their business. Walk with these items at the ready – you never know when they might be needed.

Maps

A walker without a map is like a car without a steering wheel. It is essential to obtain good maps, learn how to read and interpret them, and check your route before you set off. Most experienced walkers use a combination of maps, as described below. The sketch maps in this book are not intended to be your sole guide: use them in combination with Ordnance Survey (OS) and other maps in guide books and local publications.

Dry stone walls divide the land near the busy village of Tideswell.

The OS maps come in two main scales. First is the Landranger 1:50 000 series (about 1¼ inches to the mile). These maps cover the entire country and show footpaths, bridleways, rights of way, farm buildings, and other features. They are useful for general planning and for gaining an overall impression of the area. To cover the Peak District, Sheet Numbers 109, 110, 111, 118, 119 and 120 are needed.

The second main OS scale is 1:25 000 (roughly 2½ inches to the mile). These maps are published as individual sheets of the First and Second Series — covering the entire country, and as large fold-out Outdoor Leisure Maps for recreational areas, holiday regions, and national parks. The 1:25 000 maps are often called the 'walker's maps' because they show features important to walkers and ramblers, such as field boundaries, viewpoints, rescue posts, and rights of way. Up-to-date 1:25 000 maps are recommended for use with the maps in this book. The Outdoor Leisure Maps of the Peak District National Park are numbers 1 (The Peak District — Dark Peak Area) and 24 (The Peak District — White Peak Area).

For driving, the OS Routemaster Series, at 1:250 000 (roughly 1 inch to 4 miles) is useful, and for this area you will need Sheet 5 (Northern England). Further information is available from the Ordnance Survey.

Another useful series is the Footpath Maps published by the Ramblers Association (RA). These are at 1:25 000 scale and show many details such as footpaths, tracks, rides and bridleways, car parks and gates. For details of regions covered by these maps contact a local RA representative via a regional newspaper or community magazine, or enquire at the RA Head Office.

Safety

Most of the routes described in this book can be completed safely by the average family, provided basic safety rules are observed. In more remote country, such as the parts of the Peak District National Park, extra precautions are required (*see* below).

1 Wear suitable clothing and footwear, as described in the previous pages.
2 Always assume the weather may suddenly turn nasty. Carry an extra sweater and a waterproof, or even a small umbrella.
3 Obtain a good map and learn to read it. The maps in this book are intended for use in conjunction with detailed walkers' maps such as the Ordnance Survey 1:25 000 series.
4 On longer walks take some energy-giving food, such as chocolate or glucose lozenges, and a drink of some kind.
5 Allow plenty of time to complete your walk. A good average is 2 miles an hour — less if you enjoy views or watch nature at work.
6 If possible, have a first-aider in the group, and take change for emergency phone calls.

Safety on the Hills

Walking and scrambling in the wilder, more remote parts of our countryside can give exhilarating feelings of freedom and achievement. Tragically, more

Well Dressing

The pervious limestone of the White Peak has always given the water courses in the area an unpredictable quality. Many dales are dry and others, such as the Manifold Valley, have 'disappearing' rivers that flow one day and vanish the next. Any surface water quickly drains away, making water collection an unpredictable task.

The early inhabitants of the Peak saw the importance of a reliable water supply. Where springs did exist, these were given a mystical or supernatural quality, and offerings were bestowed in thanks for the life-giving waters. These pre-Christian rites were later revived as the elaborate flower pictures of today's well dressings.

More than twenty villages now hold well-dressing ceremonies. A wooden frame is constructed and covered with wet clay. The outline of the picture is 'pricked' into the clay's surface by the designer while other villagers collect the petals from wild and garden flowers. Many thousands of petals are collected, together with fir cones, seeds, and wool. These are then pressed into the clay to for the picture. It takes about a week to build the structure and then the heavy frame is carried carefully to the well head. The local clergyman then performs the well-blessing service, accompanied by a brass band and hundreds of visitors.

By tradition, the pictures are usually religious in character although special events, such as famine relief or an important anniversary, are sometimes celebrated.

It takes about a week's worth of patient work to 'dress' a well.

than 200 people each year set out on their last walk. Some of the fatalities are among experienced mountaineers or rock-climbers, well equipped but out on routes acknowledged to be dangerous. Yet many of those who die are ill-equipped, poorly prepared, or often just foolhardy.

Walking is supposed to be enjoyable. Among the factors that contribute to enjoyment are the knowledge and confidence that come from thorough planning, preparation, and correct equipment. None of the walks in this series is particularly hazardous or demanding, but some of the longer ones may be dangerous in poor weather or for novice walkers. Certain preparations can be life-saving, so bear in mind these points. Some of them have already been mentioned but they can not be overemphasized.

1 Be prepared. Take waterproof anorak and overtrousers, as well as a spare jumper, socks, gloves, and hat. Carry a whistle, small torch, or some other means of attracting attention, plus energy-packed food in the form of chocolate, mint cake, or glucose.
2 Detailed maps (1:25 000 or better) and compass are essential. Plan the route carefully, and bear in mind an 'escape route' to a main road, village, or rescue post in case of bad weather or injuries.
3 Check on the weather. Combine official forecasts with 'unofficial' ones from local people with good knowledge – climbers, walkers, youth hostellers, information centre staff.
4 Allow enough time for the walk, with an hour or two to spare, allowing 2 miles (3¼ km) per hour in undulating country and 1 to 1½ miles (1½-2½ km) per hour in rocky, hilly areas. Tell someone where you are going and when you expect to be back, or leave a note visible in your car.
5 The weather can close in quickly and without warning. Accept that you may have to turn back or sit tight until conditions improve; if you try to go on you may become completely lost.
6 Take a first-aid kit and know how to deal with minor injuries. Major accident victims should be kept warm and still – do not move them unless exposure is likely (*see* below). The emergency signal is six blasts on a whistle or six flashes from a torch repeated at 1-minute intervals.
7 Never walk alone. Go in threes, or better in fours. Don't separate. If there is an injury, then one or two people go for help while the rest stay with the victim.
8 Do not drink alcohol or take drugs before you set off, and make sure everyone in the party is fit enough to undertake a long walk.

Hypothermia

Hypothermia (exposure) is an insidious and dangerous condition in which body temperature falls from the normal 37 °C to 35 °C or below. It is usually caused by prolonged exposure to cold weather; it is encouraged by inadequate clothing, wet garments, high altitude, tiredness, and low temperatures (the air temperature need not be below freezing point).

The signs of hypothermia are as follows: the sufferer complains of feeling cold and is cold to the touch (even on the abdomen); he or she turns pale, shivers, and becomes irritable and irrational; as the condition worsens, the shivering stops, speech slurs, pulse slows, and the sufferer eventually loses consciousness.

When treating hypothermia, the main aim is slowly to rewarm the sufferer. Cover with warm, dry coats or blankets and move to a sheltered place. If he or she is fully conscious, provide warm, sweet drinks. Send for help and arrange a medical examination at the earliest opportunity.

KEY TO WALK MAPS

Route of walk
Main road
Other road
Footpath
Railway
Car Park
Public convenience
Information centre
Direction of walk
Castle
Camp site
Picnic site
Caravan site
Telephone
Mountain rescue centre
Mountain shelter
Youth Hostel
Monument
Viewpoint
Church
Peak / hill, outcrop
Wood
Town / building

Walk 1

THE LONGSHAW ESTATE

3 miles (5 km). Allow 1-1½ hours. Easy, with a short cut for less able walkers.

This walk offers a pleasant introduction to the Peak District through the National Trust estate at Longshaw. It is an easy ramble through pine groves, across open moorland, and finishes with a rocky stream. It is ideal for quite small children, for taking picnics, or just for a gentle afternoon's stroll. The National Trust Visitor Centre offers toilets and a café which is open during the summer months.

The walk begins from the National Trust car park at Longshaw on the B6055 close to the Fox House Inn (Grid Reference SK 267801). There is a National Trust leaflet available which describes the route through the estate.

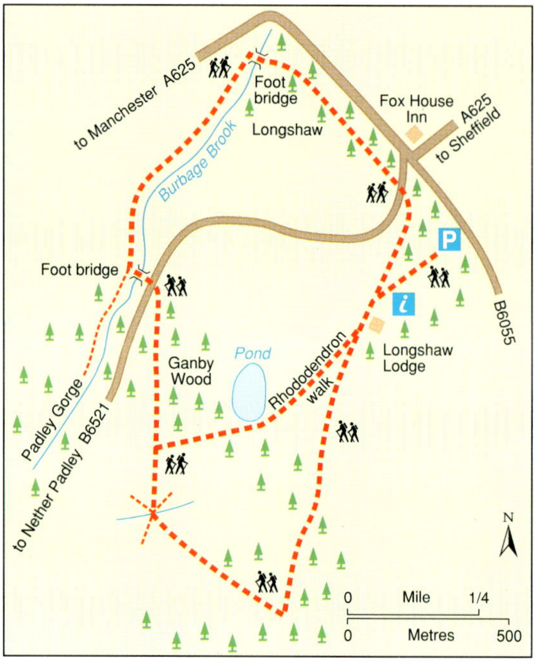

Take the grassy path past the information board down towards the visitor centre. Cross over a stone bridge, turn right, and cross over the tarmac drive to a sign marked 'FOOTPATH', and take this path alongside the wire fence. Longshaw Lodge was originally a shooting lodge for the Duke of Rutland, but it has now been converted into private apartments. On the right are the meadows where the famous Longshaw Sheepdog Trials have been held since 1898. Across the meadows on the horizon are the rocks of Owler Tor, Higger Tor, and Carl Wark.

Go through the gate ahead and straight through another gate, ignoring the track leading away to the right. Go ahead on to the wide stony track with level, easy walking. There are fine open views here through stands of oak, larch, birch, and pine. After a few minutes, look out for an old millstone lying alongside the track to the left.

(Opposite) The Longshaw Estate was acquired by the National Trust in 1927. There are views here to the Hope Valley. (Above) One of the stands of magnificent trees which grace parts of this easy walk.

Pass between the two substantial stone gate-posts. There is a fenced plantation to the left. At the end of the fence line, turn right on to a wide, grassy track and make the straight, gentle descent through the trees. Ahead is Eyam Moor with the transmitter mast on Sir William Hill. At the bottom, the tracks run off in all directions but go ahead, then right over the little stream. Climb gently and then the walk levels out past a stand of pines to your right.

Go through a gate and across a plantation of young pines to meet a well-worn path. For the shorter walk back to the visitor centre, turn right here and follow this distinct and well-signposted path. Pass by the pond and go along a rhododendron walk back to the Lodge. To continue the main route, turn left and drop down on to the road. Cross the road and go through a gate in the wall. Take the main obvious path to the right which runs down to Burbage Brook. Cross the footbridge and turn right following the worn path with the brook on your right. (By turning left after the bridge, you can make the short diversion to see the water fall into Padley Gorge.)

Continue up the path by the brook until you see a wooden bridge. Cross back over the brook and climb the stony track bearing left. Keep the brook on your left and ignore all other rough tracks. Soon the track levels out on to grass, passing through more oak, beech, and pine. Go through a little gate and on to the road. Turn right and immediately cross over to take the tarmac drive into Longshaw Lodge. In 90 metres (100 yds) you reach the Visitor Centre. The left turn takes you back to the car park.

Walk 2
THE CROMFORD CANAL

3½ miles (5½ km). Allow 2 hours. Easy, but there are some slippery woodland paths and stout shoes are needed.

This walk provides a fascinating glimpse into the industrial past at Cromford. The towpath along the canal is flat and makes for easy walking, and the return walk will take you through hillside woods and meadows.

The walk begins at Cromford Wharf, where there is ample car parking as well as toilets and refreshments during the season (Grid Reference SK 3057). For visitors by train, a short walk from Cromford Station brings you to the start.

Facing the canal, go left on to the towpath with the canal on your right. A level, twenty-minute walk brings you to the swing bridge at High Peak Junction. Cross over the bridge and visit the site with its restored workshops and information centre. Here is the start of the Sheep Pasture incline where the waggons were hauled up the hillside by winding engines.

Do not cross back over the bridge but continue along the old trackbed of the Cromford and High Peak Railway with the canal now on your left. Soon you will reach the old Transfer Shed where goods were moved from narrow boats to railway waggons. It is now used as a self-catering hostel. Pass by the shed and another smaller building on your left, and continue ahead, ignoring the road climbing off to the right. After 90 metres (100 yds), at a finger post, turn left to rejoin the canal. On the opposite side is the restored Leawood Pump Station. Cross the aqueduct over the Derwent and, at the far end, cross the little swing bridge (No 6). Go straight ahead into the trees, leaving the canal by a derelict cottage.

Cross over the railway line. The path widens at the remains of the old wharf. Pass the house on your left and find the narrow path that turns left, running between two stone walls. Turn right over a stone bridge, past the houses, and turn right on to the road. Keeping to the footpath, follow the road up into Lea Bridge and, just before the mill buildings of John Smedley, look for a hidden squeeze stile on the other side of the road. Go through the stile into Bow Wood and climb steadily up the well-trodden path. A stone wall joins the path to the right and the track levels out. In wet weather it can be slippery here. Leave the wood through a stile and on to a track which runs alongside a cottage. The path ends at a tarmac lane. Go left, down the hill keeping the wood on your right. There are fine views across the valley with the road, railway, canal, and river running in parallel. Above Cromford you can see the limestone quarries at Middleton and the loaded lorries rumbling along the A6.

About 90 metres (100 yds) past the end of the wood, go through the stile into the meadow on the right. Take a level course across to another stile in

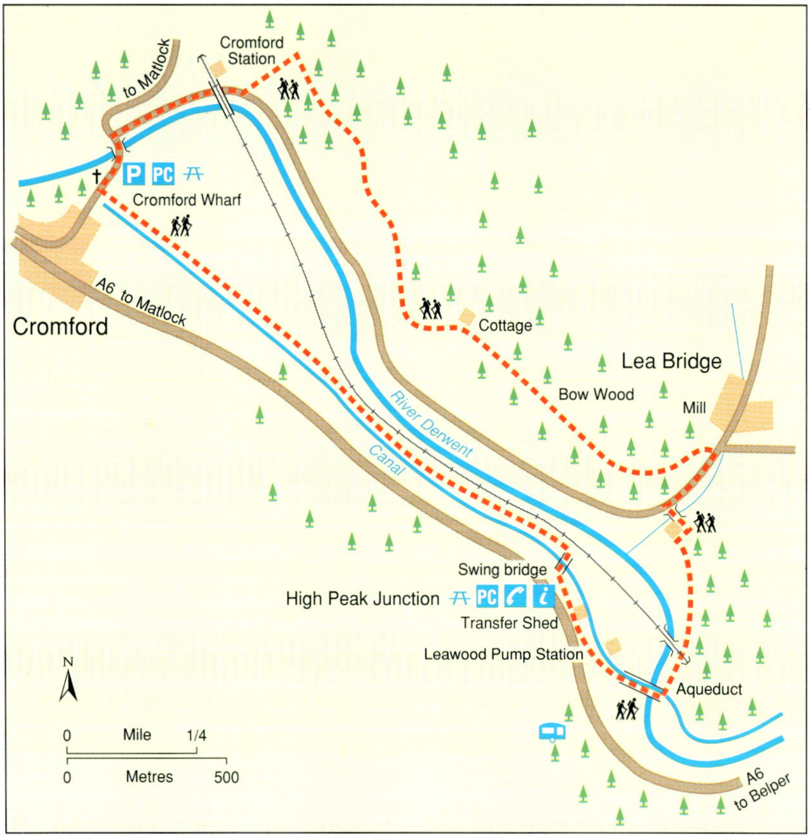

the opposite corner. Go into the next field, keeping the stone wall on your right and passing a fine oak on your left. Again, keep to a level course on a wide path. Head for two stone gate posts at the end of the wall. Go between the posts and, keeping an old hedge line to your left, aim for the middle of the wood ahead. A small stile leads into the trees. There is another wet stretch ahead, with some minor diversions because of fallen trees, but press on to where the wood opens out into another meadow.

Go through the stile, turn sharp left and descend, keeping close to the boundary fence. The path drops down on to the road through a gap in the hedge. Turn right and pass under the railway bridge. For rail travellers, the stone steps lead back to Cromford Station.

Leawood Pump House was built in 1849 to pump water from the River Derwent to supply the Cromford Canal. It has been fully restored.

To return to your car, however, continue along the road over the fifteenth-century bridge with the little ruined chapel nearby. Next to it is the seventeenth-century fishing temple with an interesting inscription above the door. About 180 metres (200 yds) further on, take the left turn back into the car park.

Walk 3

ALSTONEFIELD – HILLS AND DALES

5½ miles (9 km). Allow 2½ hours. Moderate.

Avoiding the overcrowded Dovedale, this walk is especially delightful in summer. It follows the River Dove through Wolfscote Dale and returns across walled fields to the village.

The walk begins from the village car park in Alstonefield (Grid Reference SK 131557).

From the car park, cross the road and turn right on to the path. Bear left around the cottages passing the large chestnut tree on the green to your right. Take the road ahead to Lode Mill, passing by the old Wesleyan chapel, which leads out of the village. Ignore the first track to the left and continue on for 90 metres (100 yds), taking the next left along a level stony track passing alongside a high-walled garden. Note the traditional stone barns with the 'arrowslits' in the upper levels which provided ventilation for the stored hay.

The track descends gently to the top of Gypsy Bank. Below is the River Dove and ahead the crags of Iron Tors. Bear right and go down to the river, aiming towards the building in the valley. This is an old packhorse route and you may wish to follow the zig-zag path down or make a direct descent — either way, the grass and worn rocks can be slippery. Cross the wooden footbridge and turn left into Wolfscote Dale. This is easy walking now. Look out for trout in the deep pools as well as dippers, with their white 'bibs', flying low over the water. Before the next stile, look on the right for the remains of a pump house and, just over the stile and up to the right, a stony path leads to a cave.

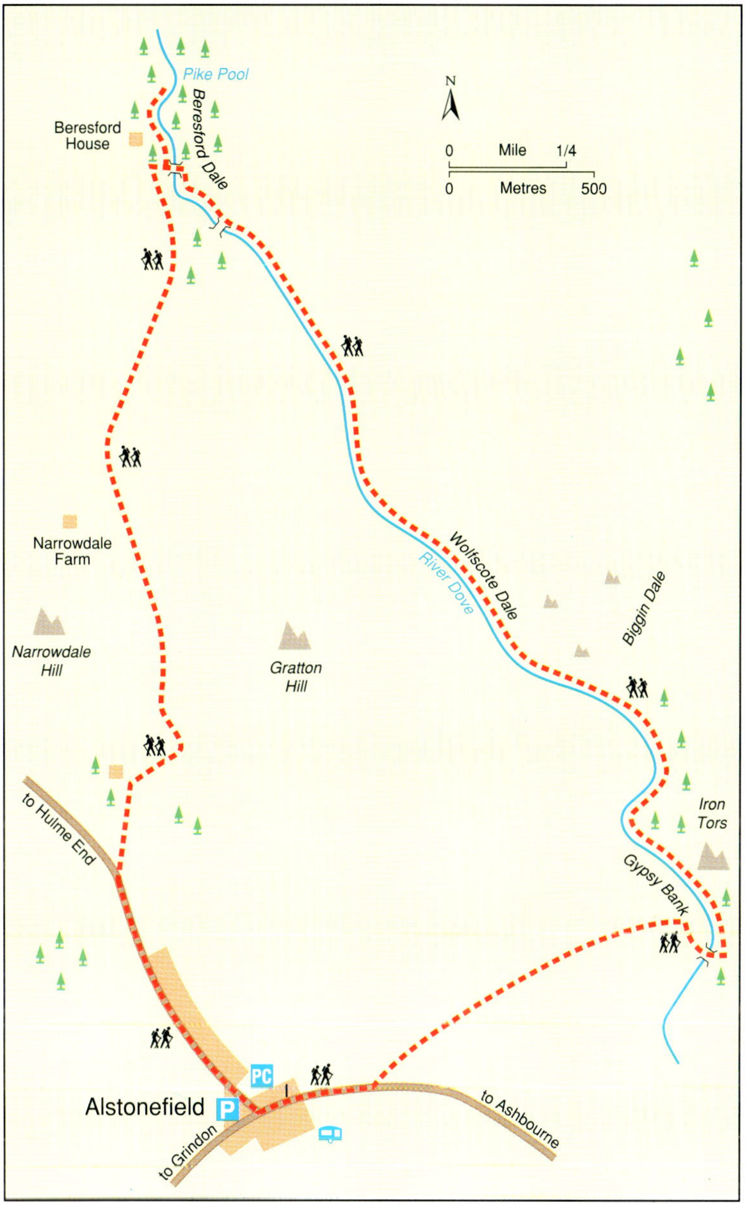

About 180 metres (200 yds) ahead, a dry valley (Biggin Dale) climbs away to the right. Here the valley is wider with the most spectacular crags towering overhead. Continue on through the dale until you come to a wooden bridge across the river. Pass by the bridge and the track rising to the right, and cross the meadow ahead. Keep to the straight path ahead to reach the river under the trees. There are three ways to cross: by the footbridge; across the stepping stones; or through the water by the ford! For a short diversion, turn right along the opposite river bank into Beresford Dale and take the ten-minute walk to the 'Pike Pool'.

Retrace your steps to the tarmac road and go ahead, leaving the river behind. Opposite the stone pillars into Beresford House, turn left through a stile into a meadow. Keep the hedge line on your right and follow it round to another stile in the corner. Keep ahead on the grassy path, climbing gently. Three more gates bring you on to a proper farm track. Where the track bends right to Narrowdale Farm, go straight ahead into the little valley, keeping on its left flank. Head towards a stone wall and a field gate and keep to the left of the enclosed fields and barn. Use the trees on the skyline as a sighting line. Cross another stile and, where the valley widens out, cross to the right flank, now keeping the wall on your left. A steady climb, still heading for the trees, takes you to a wall and track. Go right here, and through the gate into a green lane.

Continue along the level track and, before you reach the house, look for a stile in the left wall which leads diagonally to the corner of the wood. Cross two more fields by stiles to emerge on to the road. Turn left here, back into Alstonefield, passing by the pretty stone cottages and farms, all with fine views across to Hopedale. Pass the white pump on your right and follow the road back to the start.

(Opposite top) The Pike Pool in Beresford Dale is only a ten-minute diversion from the main walk. (Opposite bottom) Wolfscote Dale is far less busy than the overcrowded Dovedale and makes for easy and delightful walking, especially in the summer.

Walk 4
BAKEWELL AND MAGPIE MINE

8 miles (13 km). Allow 4 hours. Moderate.

This riverside walk to Ashford-in-the-Water provides the chance to explore the Magpie Mine. There are substantial remains to explore but keep children and dogs under control because some of the mine shafts are still accessible and dangerous. There are also some fine open views on the return section.

The walk begins from Bakewell (Grid Reference SK 2168).

Leave Bakewell via Bridge Street and cross the ancient bridge over the River Wye. Go through the little metal gate into Scott's Meadow. Follow the path through two white kissing gates into the adjoining meadow and keep ahead, aiming for the gate in the wall. Turn left on to Holme Lane and continue on passing the old packhorse bridge on the left. Keep going into the private road passing Lumford Cottages on your right. At the works, turn left and cross the bridge on to the A6.

Turn right and after 275 metres (300 yds), find a stile on your right, leading into a field and passing between houses. The path goes across the fields with the river down to the right. Just before the stone bridge, the path finally leaves the meadows through a kissing gate to rejoin the A6. Turn right and, after a few metres, bear right and cross the old bridge. Go on past the cricket pitch, crossing the main road and on into Ashford village. Keeping the Ashford Hotel on your left, turn into Church Street and continue past the church to the octagonal building (an old well) at the bottom of Fennel Street.

Turn left over the old sheepwash bridge to rejoin the A6. Cross over and turn right, following the main road for about 180 metres (200 yds). Take the minor road left, signposted to Sheldon, and, where the road begins the climb, go right over a stile leading to the riverside path. Ignore the obvious level path alongside the river and take the path that climbs up left to a broken wall on the skyline. The route is not obvious here but, on nearing this wall, veer away left, keeping this wall on your right.

Still climbing, make for a dip in the skyline (with the river valley behind) and the gradient becomes less steep. Soon the path runs close to Shacklow Wood on your right passing through three more stiles. The woods drop away to the right but stay level and head towards the house. Join the road by a stile just to the left of this house. Turn right into Sheldon village. Just past the first house on the left, take the footpath that leads into the field. Cross two more stiles while keeping the wall to your right. Cross another field, aiming for a third stile and now keep the wall on your left. A fourth stile and a diagonal path lead directly to the buildings of Magpie Mine.

Retrace your steps to the low circular building (the old powder house) and head into the corner of the enclosure to a stile. Cross the stile and bear right keeping alongside the wall. After 180 metres (200 yds), take the squeeze stile in the wall into the adjoining field. Turn left and keep to the left side of the field to come to a walled green lane which descends to the road in Kirkdale. Cross the road and, immediately opposite, cross the stile and climb up aiming for the right-hand end of the trees on the skyline.

Cross a stile in the trees, turn right, and, after 10 metres (just over 10 yds), go over a stone stile into a field. Turn left, diagonally across the field, to a marker post and a stile in the fence line. Cross this and bear left, keeping the fence line to your left. Look ahead to a small building with a corrugated iron roof and, on the skyline, the television mast on Stanton Moor. This will be your sighting line all the way to Over Haddon village. You will find the next stile in the corner of the field, hidden by trees.

Now, using the TV mast for direction, cross three more fields with stiles to join the Bakewell to Monyash road. Turn right for about 20 metres (22 yds) and cross over into another field just before Melbourne Farm. Take a diagonal course to the opposite corner by the trees and continue to the corner of the next field. Go over another stile and bear half-right, keeping close to the wall on your left. Two-thirds of the way down, cross the wall by a stile and again use the mast for a direction. The next stile is just to the left of a prominent water trough. Directly ahead and in line, is the village of Over Haddon. The path descends diagonally across this next field, and the

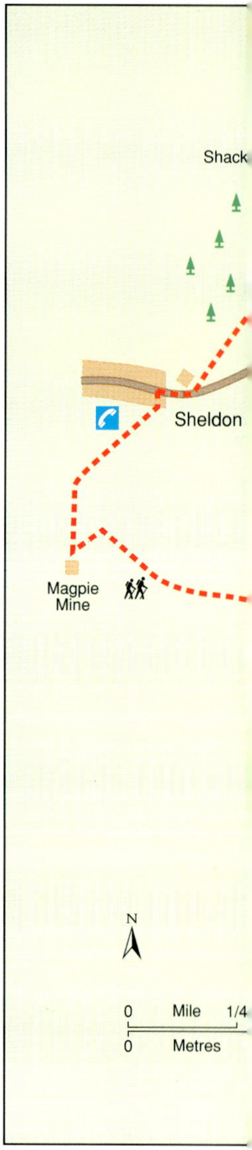

next stile is 90 metres (100 yds) below a solitary hawthorn tree set against the wall. Follow this diagonal path, still keeping the sighting line, towards the village. In the field just before the new farmhouse, find the little stile in the right-hand wall and drop down the side of the field heading for the trees and farm buildings.

A stile leads to the road. Turn left and pass through the village, keeping straight ahead to the T-junction. Turn left to Bakewell. Out of the village, ignore the right turn to Youlgreave and continue on the level road. Where the road curves left, go ahead through a stile down into a dip and climb again, rejoining the road at a hidden stile by a dewpond. Turn right and pass by the track to Burton Manor Farm. After the S-bend, find another hidden stile to the right and drop down the field passing by mature ash trees. A diagonal path leads to a double stile. Take the first stile but then bear right towards the school buildings. Head towards the left corner over another stile into another field. Again, head for the corner and into the school grounds with the buildings on the right. Cross the road into the playing fields.

At the corner, ignore the path right into the houses and go straight ahead, aiming for a stone building in the corner. Go through one last stile and on to a tarmac path called The Yeld. Continue on, descending and turning right to join Yeld Road. Take a sharp left and then right into Monyash Road. Still descending, return to the town centre at Rutland Square.

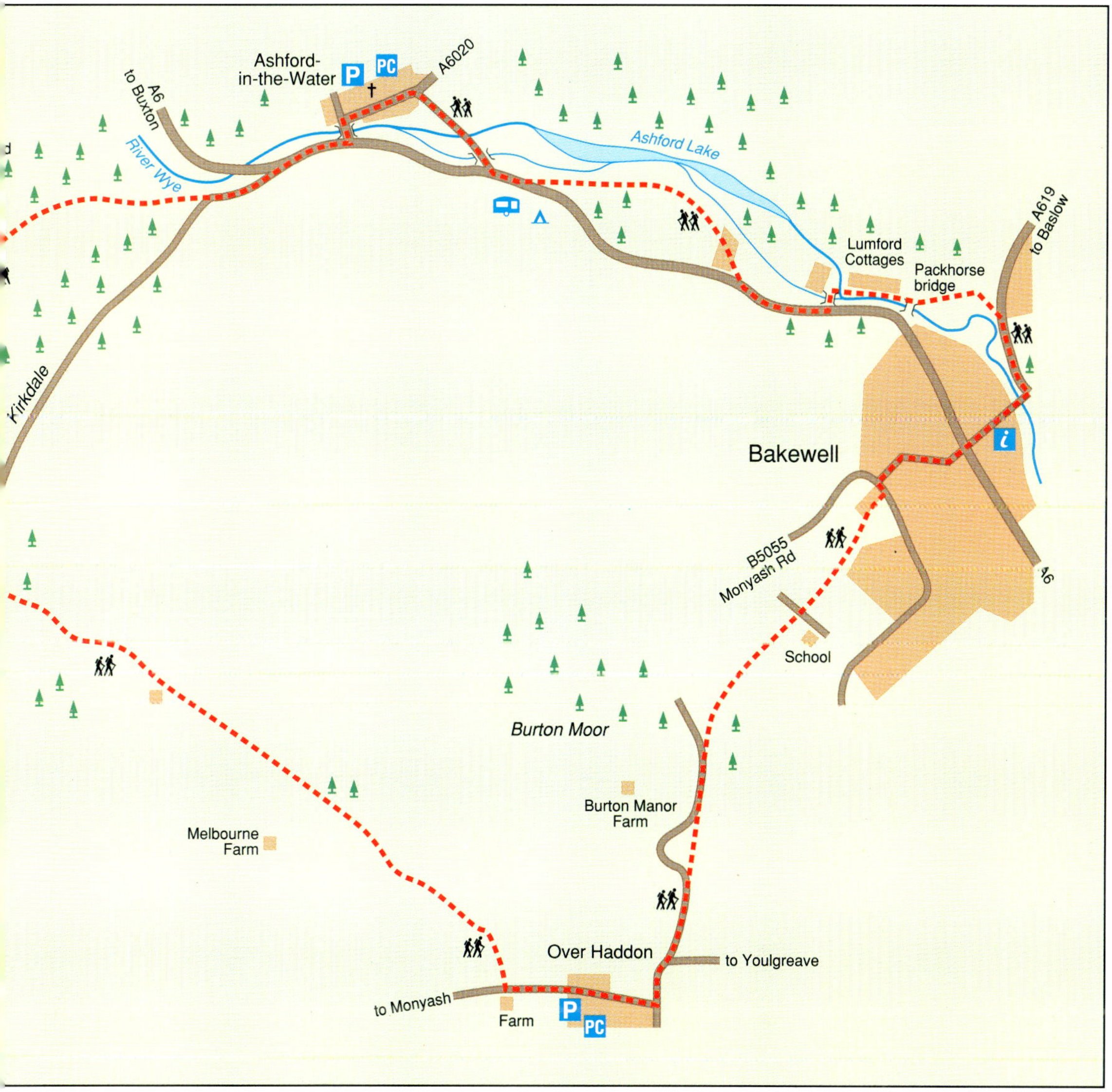

Walk 5

BRETTON AND ABNEY CLOUGH

5 miles (8 km). Allow 3-4 hours. Moderate but with a short, steep ascent of Bretton Clough.

This is a fine walk across open moorland. There are wooded cloughs as well as an inn with a view!

The walk begins from the Bretton end of Sir William Hill where you can park the car (Grid Reference SK 210770).

Take the stony track towards the transmitter mast and go over the summit of Sir William Hill passing the mast to your right. After 180 metres (200 yds), go over the stile left on to the open heather moor. The path is clear and takes a level course ahead. At the high point near the disturbed ground, pause to enjoy the views.

Take the path straight ahead, with the mast at your left shoulder, descending past waymarks to the stile next to a gate. Go over the stile and take the wide grassy path downwards, keeping the wall on your right. There are good views of Bretton Clough to the left. Cross another stile keeping to the easy path. Soon the wall curves away right and the path drops towards the trees. The path zig-zags to reach Bretton Brook at Stoke Ford. Keep to the well-worn, sunken path. The ford has disappeared and walkers now have a dry crossing over a little footbridge and a stile. Turn right to cross a second footbridge leading to a junction of paths a few metres ahead. Take the left path into the trees, and start the gentle climb into Abney Clough under a canopy of oak, ash, rowan, and larch.

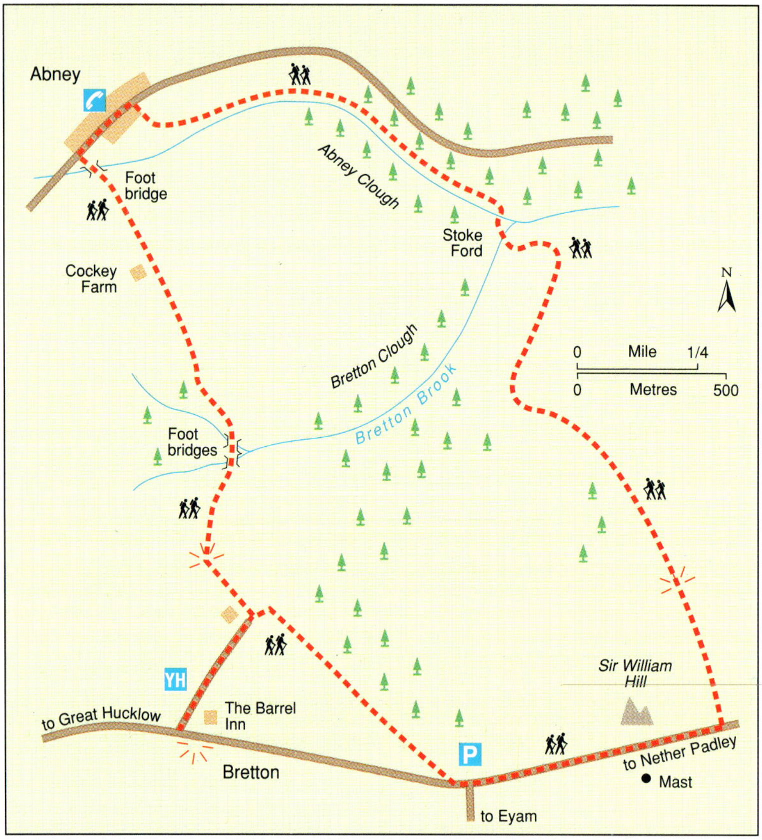

Soon the valley opens up leaving the denser woodland behind. The path is easy to follow and finally leads out into the hamlet of Abney via a metal farm gate. Turn left and walk on past the farms and cottages, looking out for the telephone box on the left. About 20 metres (22 yds) past the box, take the path over the stile into the field to cross a stream by a little footbridge. Climb up the steps to a gate in a boundary fence. Go through and turn left, following the fence line. Cross the farm track and go on up into the open field. Ahead is Cockey Farm. Head towards the left side of the farmhouse by way of two stiles.

Keep to the farm track, passing the farm on your right. Where the track turns left, bear right following signs to a stile. Cross, and keep the field wall to your left. Go over another stile and the path begins to drop

(Opposite) *Sunlight dapples the ground in Abney Clough. (Above) A snowscape view from Bretton Edge near the Barrel Inn, Derbyshire's highest pub. (Below) A clough is a narrow valley, and there are fine views of Bretton Clough from this walk.*

down to the trees. One more stile to the left, and the path descends into Bretton Clough through bracken and trees. Cross the footbridge and another stile. Cross a second bridge and the well-defined path begins immediately to climb away from the stream.

The path heads up towards the skyline. A marker post points the way. There is a steep section here with steps to a stile. Pause for breath and look back at the view. Go through the stile and keep straight ahead, less steeply now, to another stile set in the corner of the field. Cross the stile keeping the wall on your right. Go through another stile and look for the house ahead. Aim towards the left of the house and a stile in the garden wall which leads past the house, to the tarmac road. Turn right and follow the road to the hamlet of Bretton. There are fine views from Derbyshire's highest pub, The Barrel Inn, dating from 1637 and situated at 378 metres (1240 ft).

For a quick return to the starting point, leave the inn, turn left, and the road takes you directly back to Sir William Hill. Otherwise, retrace your steps back to the house and continue along the tarmac track. Pass another house on the left, and the track becomes stony. Continue ahead, crossing another track by a plantation of pines. Soon the track emerges on to the road and a left turn leads directly to the starting point.

Walk 6
KINDER VIEWS

5 miles (8 km). Allow 3 hours. Moderate.

This is a walk to the fringes of the high moorland below Kinder. It returns on the ancient packhorse route by the banks of the River Sett.

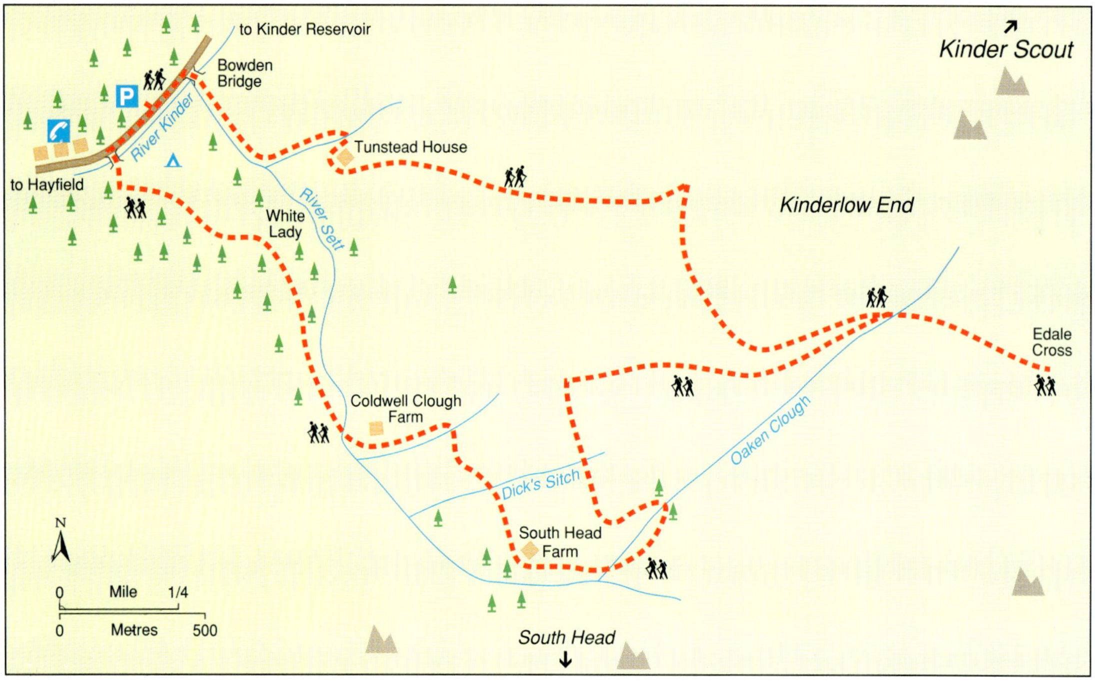

The walk begins from the Bowden Bridge car park, a mile (1.6 km) east from Hayfield, on the Kinder Road (Grid Reference SK 049869).

From the old quarry car park, cross over the bridge, turn left and follow the road alongside the river for 90 metres (100 yds). Where the road bends to the right, you can see the old packhorse bridge (Bowden Bridge) that crosses the River Kinder. Continue along the road, passing over a bridge. The little River Sett is now on your right. Just before the road bears right over another bridge, take the stony track, by a metal gate, to Tunstead House. The track climbs and curves to the right, around the side of the farmyard. Still climbing, pass by the front of the house and continue up the walled track to cross several fields and stiles. Ignore the waymarked signpost that points right and continue straight on uphill to the stile set in the wall. Aim for the rounded hill of Kinderlow End on the skyline. As you climb, you will see to your left the western slopes of Kinder Scout and, if the weather is clear, the waterfall at Kinder Downfall.

The path finally comes out at the edge of the enclosed fields, by a stile and a gate, on to the open moorland. Go ahead for 18 metres (20 yds) to find a broad, defined path. Turn left and 135 metres (150 yds) ahead are a wire boundary fence and stile. **Do not** cross but turn sharp right to take the well-worn, level path that runs below the flank of Kinderlow End. In misty or low cloud conditions, make sure you stay on the path because any deviations to the left will lead you up on to the Kinder plateau. On the skyline, directly ahead, is the rounded top of South Head. Soon, you will come to a junction of paths. Take the upper, left, path that climbs over the shoulder of the hill ahead. This path climbs and curves around the lower grassy slopes of Kinderlow End. The hilltop of South Head should now be on your right.

You are now on a level course and the path leads, by way of a stile, to a stony track climbing up out of Oaken Clough. This is the Edale Road, the continuation of the packhorse route from Bowden Bridge via Jacob's Ladder (*See* Walk 8.) If you have the energy, turn left and a twenty-minute walk up the track will take you to the summit at Edale Cross, with views to the southern slopes of Kinder. Retrace your steps to the stile.

Alternatively, turn right and take the track down the hill with Oaken Clough on your left and a stone wall to the right. Continue down the track to pass through a wide gate by the National Trust Kinder sign. Soon you will come to a wooden fence with a gate and stile. Go over the stile and turn left, leaving the track, across another stile into a field. Keep close to the fenceline and head for another stile, left, into the adjacent field. Now keep the wall on your right. Cross another stile at a boggy patch and, keeping the wall on the right, cross the field to a stile which leads into Oaken Clough. The path runs through the trees ahead, passing a derelict shooting cabin, and turns right over a culvert to contour around the hillside. Follow the waymarked path down to join a stony farm track. Turn right and take the track, crossing two more stiles, to the trees ahead at South Head Farm. Go through the farmyard and continue along the track.

Where the track crosses Dick's Sitch ('sitch' means damp or marshy place), there is new tree planting — one of the National Trust's new woodland conservation areas. Just over the cattle grid, the track turns left, over a stream, to rejoin the Edale Road. Pass Coldwell Clough Farm and drop down to continue alongside the River Sett. Ahead are two gates. Go through the left gate and take the road that climbs up out of the valley. Near the top of the hill, ignore the first bridleway off to the left, and continue to the old guide post known as the 'White Lady'. Now leave the road to take this bridleway to the left, signposted to Stubbs Piece and Highgate.

(Above) Kinder Reservoir, with Kinder Scout beyond, in winter. (Below) A view from the rounded top of South Head showing most of the walk.

Go through the bridle gate and, where the tracks diverge either side of the plantation, take the lower path that runs beside the trees. Passing the house and field on your right, look for a small stile and turn right through the trees to descend a flight of stone steps. Cross the campsite through two gates, and cross the river ahead. Turn right at the iron railings and climb up to the road. Cross over and turn right to return to the car park.

Walk 7

THE DANE VALLEY

7½ miles (12 km). Allow 4½ hours. Moderate.

This route makes a near-perfect all-day summer walk, and it includes farmland with views, three interesting inns, and a cool, shady walk in the Dane Valley.

The walk begins from the layby at Brookside, south-west of Wildboarclough (Grid Reference SJ 981682).

With the brook on your left, turn left over the bridge and immediately turn right on to a footpath through the trees. Cross a stile and go out into the field keeping close to the fenceline. Cross the next stile and head towards the trees following the yellow waymarks. Pass by the derelict farm buildings and take the green track curving around to the left. Pass the second group of buildings and take the high stile to the right, signposted to Owlers Bridge. Cross the field, keeping to the right, to a stile and a footbridge in the trees. Cross Clough Brook and turn left on to the road. After 90 metres (100 yds), take the track off to the right which leads to Hammerton Knowl Farm. From the field, there are good views back towards Wildboarclough while, to the south-east, you can see the craggy outline of the Roaches.

(Below) The walk circles Allgreave seen here from Hammerton Knowl. (Bottom) Contented horses graze in a rich meadow along the way.

Follow the track as it swings away left, past the farm buildings, and strike off half-right to a stile that can be seen on the skyline. Cross over and go ahead, keeping to the lower part of the field. With the line of a derelict wall on your left, cross the fields by the stiles, until you see the roof line of the Wild Boar Inn. Head for the left side and come out on to the road. Opposite the front of the inn, cross over to two field gates. Go through the left gate on to a grassy track. Take a level course with the trees to the left and the clough on the right. Keep to the right of a stone wall and a line of young planted trees until you reach the end of the field. Go through a field gate to join a concrete farm road. Take the road downhill and, where the road bends right. Go straight ahead, down a sunken muddy track.

At Hammerton Farm, turn right on to the road and, after 45 metres (50 yds), turn left into a field next to a bungalow. Head towards the bottom of the field where a stile can be seen. Cross over and, after 45 metres (50 yds), cross the brook to another stile. Cross and go half-left, keeping to the lower part of the field. Cross the stile in the trees ahead, crossing the farm entrance to another stile and field gate. Go across the field to another stile in the opposite wall by the large trees. Turn right to a kissing gate, down the stone steps, and turn left on to the road. Pass the old Ship Inn and the cottages to cross the river at Dane Bridge. Immediately past the Staffordshire boundary sign, take the footpath left to Gradbach. Ahead there is a delightful 2½-mile (4-km) walk along the Dane Valley, through damp woodlands and over open fields with the river running through the gorge below.

The path begins close to the river, crosses a meadow, and heads up to the right into the first of several woodlands. The winding path climbs up through the trees to come out at open fields, where the river lies 180 metres (200 yds) down to the left. To the left can be seen the rounded summit of Shutlingsloe. Pass Back Dane Farm and keep to the stony track. Where the track climbs away to the right, take the level path ahead through the field littered with boulders. Pass by a derelict farm and follow the path as it drops down towards the river. Go over the stile, passing the Roaches Estate sign, to enter another fine stretch of mixed woodland.

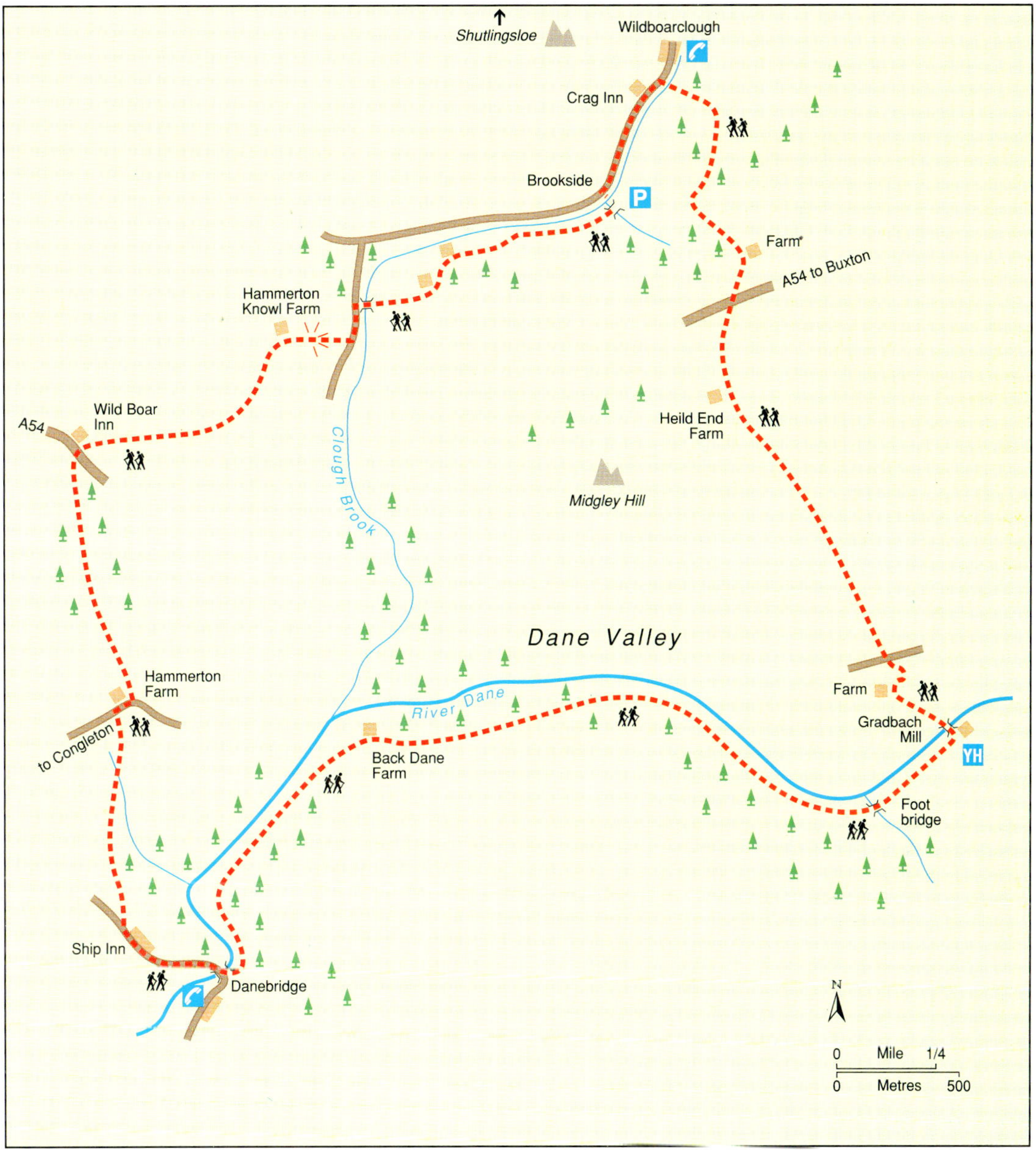

The path drops down to an open meadow by the river, overhung by large beech trees. Turn left over the footbridge, signposted to Gradbach, and climb the track for about 18 metres (20 yds). Take the stile to the left set in the wall. Cross, and take the lower, left track that runs close to the river by a fenceline. Take the stile to the right and follow the path that leads out to Gradbach Mill, now a youth hostel. Turn left in front of the mill building and cross the footbridge to a track that climbs up to the left. Cross the field littered with rocks, passing the farm to the left. Join the farm track and continue uphill to the road. Cross over and take the stony track ahead. Keep to the track, and continue via the field gates, to the top of the rise.

The track descends to join the farm road from Heild End and, where the road turns sharply to the left, go ahead to the stile and cross the main A54 Congleton-Buxton road. Take the opposite stile and head for the group of trees and farm buildings. Turn left in front of the barn and take a diagonal course to the right of the conifer plantation. Cross the next stile which leads to a muddy, sunken path running down beside another wood. At the field, bear left to take a waymarked diagonal course to a boggy stream. Avoid the wet and continue down the line of trees to a stile at the edge of the wood. Take the path down through the trees which emerges to cross a footbridge over Clough Brook. Go left on to the road past the Crag Inn and, a few minutes later, you arrive back at the layby.

Walk 8

KINDER SCOUT AND EDALE

8 miles (13 km). Allow 5 hours. Difficult.

Following the Pennine Way National Trail on to the southern edge of Kinder, the walk returns via the old packhorse route into the Edale Valley.

The walk begins from the main car park near Edale railway station (Grid Reference SK 124853).

From the car park, go under the railway bridge and take the road up into Grindsbrook Booth. Pass by the Peak National Park information centre at Fieldhead on the way. At the famous Nags Head, the Pennine Way begins its 250-mile (400-km) route to the Scottish border. Pass to the left of the inn and follow the stony track to the Lodge. Take the waymarked path off to the right as it drops down to cross the brook by a log bridge. Climb the steps and turn left into the meadow to join the Pennine Way.

Keep to the level and well-worn path across Grindsbrook Meadows and do not take the path right which climbs up the hillside. The path continues through a wood to emerge at Golden Clough where you cross the stream on a footbridge. Over the bridge, start the steady climb up into Grindsbrook Clough. The path ahead can be seen curving away left. Keep to the path with the stream running down below on your left. A twenty-minute steady walk brings you to a jumble of boulders known as 'Halfway House'. Scramble over these to get back on the path. The valley narrows here and, ahead on the skyline, is the steep rocky cleft that will be the way out on to the plateau. Soon the path crosses the stream and reaches a junction of two valleys. Ignore the larger valley to the right and keep left where the path becomes steep and rough. A 180-metre (200-yd) scramble leads up on to the Kinder plateau.

The charming packhorse bridge at the foot of Jacob's Ladder.

Take care here because there are various paths that lead off in all directions. With the stream bed on your right, find the cairn of stones and take a course westwards (half-left) following a boggy path across the peat. Head for a group of rocks on the skyline. At these rocks, the route ahead can be seen clearly. The wide path follows the southern edge of the plateau, by Crowden Tower, through the boulder fields of the 'Woolpacks' to the whaleback spur of the Swine's Back. Here the path is easy walking and soon drops down to cross the stream at the head of Crowden Clough. Bear left and take the short, steep climb to the imposing outcrop of Crowden Tower. From the top, the path leads on to the wind-sculpted rock garden of the 'Woolpacks'. Take time to explore these strange, eroded forms.

Return to the path and keep on a westerly course, passing by the Noe Stool on your left and, up to the right, the jutting outcrop of Edale Rocks. There are fine views down the valley to Lee Farm and Upper Booth. The path runs to the foot of the Swine's Back where a broad path drops away left. Ignore this and continue on the level path that contours around the hillside following a broken-down wall. The path turns left and drops down to a stile at Edale Cross. Turn left on to the stony track. This is the old packhorse route from Hayfield into Edale. Go ahead over the stile in the

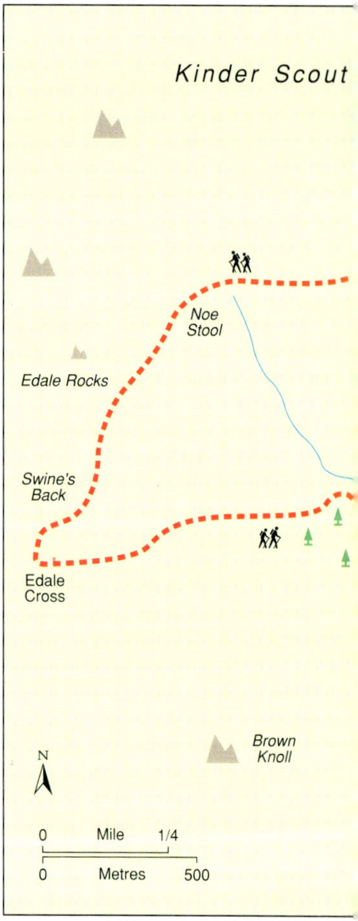

boundary wall and continue straight ahead on the track that now begins the descent. Much of the track has been repaired in the traditional way using stone setts and, although it is steep in places, the walking is fairly easy. Towards the valley bottom, the track divides, with the old packhorse route off to the right, or Jacob's Ladder (path) to the left. Take either because both routes meet at the packhorse bridge.

Cross the bridge and continue along the track past Lee Farm where there is a National Trust Information point in an old barn. Cross the stone bridge at Upper Booth and, opposite the telephone box, turn left into the farmyard and follow the footpath signs to the right to Grindsbrook Booth. Follow the wire fence and then strike off half-left uphill towards some trees and a derelict barn. Bear right to take the path that runs through the hillocks of the Broadlee Bank landslip. Continue across fields making a gentle descent towards the village. At the final stile, turn right into the sunken and shady Peat Lane which brings you out at the Nags Head. Turn right and follow the road back to the car park.

The rocky ravine of Grindsbrook Clough near the start of the walk.

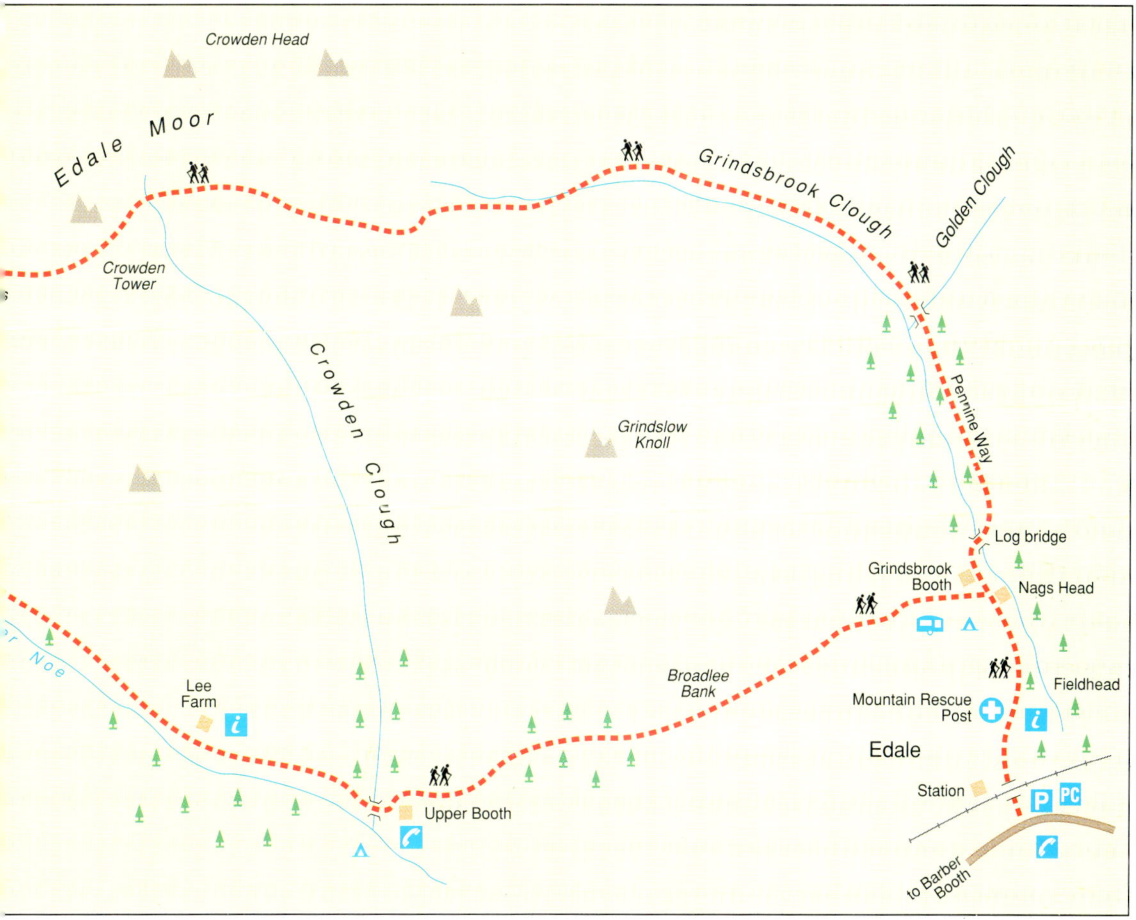

Drive 1

THE 'WELL DRESSING' VILLAGES

40 miles (64 km). Allow 2-3 hours, at least, and all day if you wish to visit the wells or other sites mentioned.

A tour around the limestone plateau, passing through the more popular 'well dressing' villages, steeped in customs, traditions and history. There are some narrow, twisting lanes but moderate gradients.

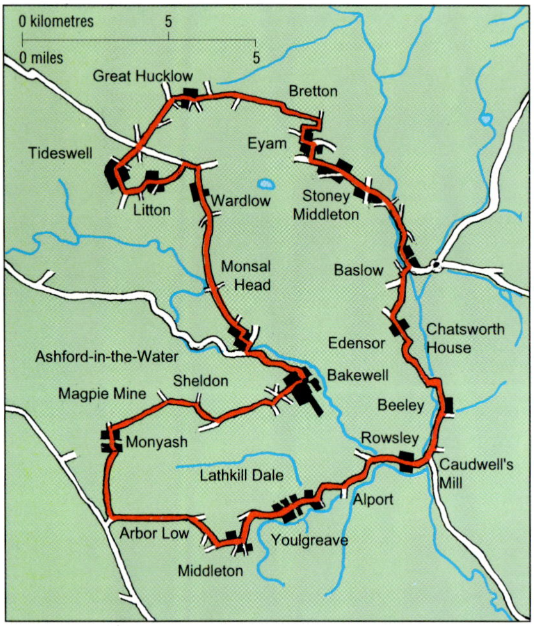

This tour starts in Bakewell with plenty of pay and display parking, although much reduced on Monday (market day).

From the roundabout in Rutland Square, take the B5055 to Monyash passing to the left of the Rutland Arms Hotel. With the Old Market Hall and parish church on your right, wind your way up out of the town on to the limestone plateau. The road levels out providing wide views on either side. After 2 miles (3 km), prepare for a partially hidden right turn signposted to Sheldon, Flagg, and Chelmorton. Turn here and drive on. Take a sharp bend to the left leading to a straight and level run.

Astonishingly, a Cornish tin mine chimney and engine house appear on the right. This windswept and atmospheric site contains the preserved remains of 'Magpie Mine' where lead was extracted.

In 180 metres (200 yds), the road bends to the right where you take the left fork down Horse Lane. Sweeping views of the White Peak open up with Monyash nestling in the hollow. Turn left at the T-junction into the village and continue ahead to the crossroads at the green. Go straight ahead signposted to Newhaven and Youlgreave.

A steady climb for 1½ miles (2½ km) carries you back up on to the plateau. Over the crest, look for a left turn to Youlgreave and Arbor Low. In a couple of minutes you will pass the track leading to Arbor Low, a Neolithic stone circle consisting of sixty fallen slabs.

Shortly the road is joined on the right by a narrow band of trees and disturbed ground. This is Long Rake, a former lead vein worked for several miles but subsequently abandoned. Nowadays the ground is reworked for fluorspar, used in steelmaking.

Take the next right fork signposted to Middleton and White Peak Scenic Route and after, 450 metres (500 yds) go straight across the crossroads. Drop gently down, turning left towards Middleton by Youlgreave. At the next T-junction bear right. Ahead is Youlgreave, clinging to the side of the dale. There are some fine buildings here including the old Co-op, now a youth hostel. Keeping the church on your right, head out on the same road. At the edge of the village the road drops down towards Alport. D.H. Lawrence country this, with Lathkill Dale on your left. Both Youlgreave and Alport were used as film settings in *The Virgin and the Gipsy*.

The solid-looking bridge attests to Bakewell's importance as a crossing point of the the River Wye.

After Alport, the road winds its way along the dale with glimpses of the River Bradford. Take care past the quarry and blind corner junction which follows, but stay on this course until you reach the main A6. A right, straight on to a short dual carriageway to Matlock brings you quickly into the pretty village of Rowsley with Caudwell's Mill, a restored and working flour mill, and the Peacock Hotel, a fine coaching inn.

After 450 metres (500 yds), the main road takes a sharp right but you take the left turning to Baslow (B6012). Passing by Beeley village on the right, the road snakes its way though the Derwent valley. Fine woodland views and neat hedgerows herald the way into Chatsworth Park. A sharp left and an incongruous set of traffic lights lead you over a fine eighteenth-century bridge over the River Derwent. Open parkland lies ahead. There are fine views of Chatsworth House to the right, but look out for deer and sheep which roam freely. Edensor church spire rises above the trees ahead. Continue through the park, finally passing over a cattle grid at Edensor village with its fine architectural oddities.

Stay on this road until you reach Baslow. At the roundabout, take the left to Stockport and Manchester (A623) and continue on to Calver. High to your right are the gritstone crags of Froggatt and Curbar Edges. At Calver traffic lights, continue on to Stoney Middleton 1 mile (1½ km) ahead, set in a narrow defile between towering limestone cliffs. After 1 mile (1½ km) make a right turn to Eyam (B6521) climbing and winding up the side dale until you reach Eyam Square. A sharp left brings you into the main street past the church and Plague Cottage. Take the next right turn into Hawkhill Road. Continue up Hawkhill Road with views down to Eyam. The road narrows and twists, finally emerging at a junction. Make the left turn here to Bretton and Great Hucklow. This is the start of a 3-mile (5-km) ridge road with tantalizing views to the south and a promise of more to come. Go through a series of bends then on towards the Barrel Inn. There are views south across the limestone plateau and north to Kinder and the northern moors. Shortly after the Inn, the road divides. Take the high road right to Great Hucklow.

A lovely picture adorns a well head in thanks for the life-giving gift of water.

The road drops down from the ridge into Great Hucklow. Through the village, over the crossroads, and join the B6049 left to Tideswell. Another 1½ miles (2½ km) of straight road ahead ends at a staggered crossroads. Take care with a right on to the A623 followed by a left to Tideswell. Immediately the church, aptly named the Cathedral of the Peak, appears above the rooftops. Drop down into the village keeping to the through route which opens up into a wide thoroughfare. Continue out of the village and, when the last houses are past, prepare to take a left turn to Litton. Go up through Litton Dale into the tree lined village. A mile (1½ km) on, rejoin the A623 with a right turn. Look out for 'Peters Stone', a limestone outcrop on your right.

At the bottom of the hill, leave the main road with a right turn to Wardlow (B6465). A steady climb takes you through Wardlow and up on to the crest of the hill. Stop at Monsal Head for a look at the elegant Monsal Viaduct over the River Wye. Make the gentle descent for 1 mile (1½km) to Ashford. At the next obvious split in the road, take the right fork to Buxton (A6) passing the Ashford village sign on your left. Enter the village down into Fennel Street where the road bends left. Visit the sheepwash bridge.

Go along the main street for 275 metres (300 yds) and bear right to a T-junction. Turn right and, after 180 metres (200 yds), turn left on to the A6 back to Bakewell in time for tea and a Bakewell Pudding!

The magnificent Chatsworth House was built in the seventeenth century.

Drive 2
THE NORTHERN MOORS

67 miles (108 km). Allow 3-4 hours.

This is the classic drive over the most spectacular passes and northern moors, including the dramatic Winnatts Pass. There are some severe gradients with tight corners, and roads can be impassable in winter conditions. This drive may be completed at its best in late autumn.

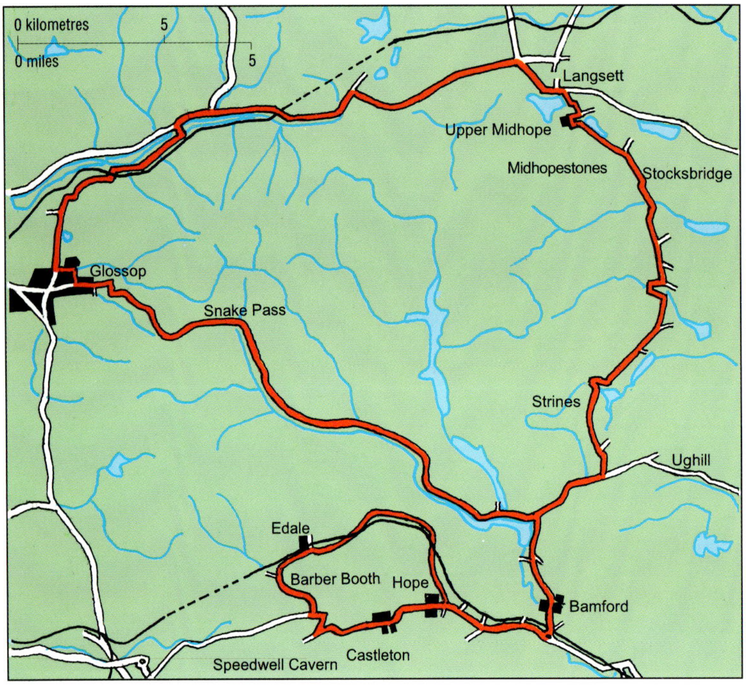

From the main car park in Castleton turn right, away from the village. After 275 metres (300 yds), look for the left turn to Speedwell Cavern. [The main road ends ½ mile (800 m) on.] Climb up this lane to the foot of Winnatts Pass with Speedwell Cavern on your left. Pass over the cattle grid and on up the steep pass with the overhanging crags. The road levels and passes over another cattle grid to arrive at a junction. Turn sharp right to Chapel-en-le-Frith. 'Mam Tor' lies ahead. Negotiate a sharp left on the A625 and, after 275 metres (300 yds) make a hairpin right signposted to Barber Booth and Edale.

Go up to the crest at 'Mam Nick' and over into Edale. Panoramic views open up before you: Edale valley head, Kinder Scout with Edale village nestling below, and the Pennine Way snaking up out of Grindsbrook. The road winds down the side of the valley and, after a final long, straight descent, turns right to follow the dale eastwards to Hope village. After ¾ mile (1.2 km), look out for the left turn to Edale village if you want to visit. Continue on the road to Hope winding through this beautiful valley with the slopes of Kinder on your left, and Lose Hill, Back Tor, and Mam Tor to the right. The end of the valley drive is signalled by a switchback across a narrow stone bridge. Houses line the road now and soon Hope church stands at the T-junction.

Turn left here on to the A625 to Sheffield. After 2 miles (3 km) look out for a petrol station and make a left to Bamford and Ladybower on the A6013. Drive up into the village with the crags of Bamford Edge rising above. Carry on for 1½ miles (2.4 km) and the road passes alongside Ladybower Reservoir at the dam at Yorkshire Bridge. The wooded flank of Win Hill drops into the water to the left. The viaduct ahead ends at a T-junction, so turn right on to the A57 to Sheffield.

After 2 miles (3 km), take the next left to Strines. Go over the cattle grid ignoring the right to Ughill. After the Strines Inn, the road narrows and care is needed on the next section with its steep gradients and narrow turns. The first drop-and-turn passes through woodlands but soon the view, right, opens up with glimpses of High and Low Bradfield. Eventually the road makes a hard turn to the left signposted to Midhopestones and Penistone. Ignore the turn to the right marked Bradfield. A level course

The towers of Alport Castles are purely natural features.

The dramatic gorge of the Winnatts Pass is owned by the National Trust and has been designated a Site of Special Scientific Interest.

ahead but soon there is another plunge into a wooded valley and a sharp right over a stone bridge. Climbing again following Midhopestones, the road reaches a summit with views in all directions. Go over the top and the road stretches ahead. Ignore the right turn to Bradfield and make the gentle descent. Ignore another right to Bolsterstone and keep the boundary wall enclosing woodland to your right, with the open moor on your left. Soon, another stone wall runs on the left and the road once again falls into a third wooded valley with another right over a stone bridge.

After 90 metres (100 yds) there is a severe hairpin left on a 1 in 5 incline. A stiff climb for ½ mile (0.8 km) is rewarded by emerging views to the moors across isolated farmsteads. At last, go over the hill and carry straight on passing the junction right to Bolsterstone and Stocksbridge. After a gentle descent for ⅔ mile (1 km), take a left turn. This may be unmarked. The road ahead is edged to the right with conifer plantations with moorland to the left. Soon you reach the little hamlet of Upper Midhope at the hill top. After the stone cottages, the road turns to the left and is hemmed in by stone walls. It is signed to Langsett. Go over Langsett Reservoir, across the dam wall into the village. At the T-junction, turn left on to the A616 to Huddersfield. This is the end of the minor roads. After 1 mile (1.6 km) at a major crossroads, turn left again on to the A628 to Manchester.

Over the county boundary, back into Derbyshire, the road begins the descent into Longdendale. Look to the left for the first electricity pylon. The cables emerge from the western entrance of the Woodhead tunnel, once an important trans-Pennine rail link. Go over a concrete bridge and the road from Holme joins from the right. Ahead on the skyline is a little chapel. Take a rather sudden left to Glossop (B6105) which runs to the other side of the valley. Here, the road keeps company with the pylons and old railway trackbed. Drive on over the brow and you have a long straight run towards Glossop with views of Kinder ahead. After 180 metres (200 yds) beyond the 30 mph sign, turn left into Church Street. Go down the hill into Old Glossop past a fine terrace of cottages and swing round the church on your right. Carry on to the T-junction and a left to Sheffield. This is the infamous Snake Pass, your route back over the moors. Continue past the golf course, and immediately you are up on wild and open moorland. Drive on to the summit noting the guide posts that mark the line of the road in deep snow.

Descend, gently at first, into the Woodlands Valley, passing the Snake Inn on your left. The road takes an undulating course for 5-6 miles (8-9 km) with fine views of the northern slopes of Kinder. Pass by the left turn to Derwent Valley, go over the viaduct and, after 1 mile (1.6 km), make the right turn to Bamford on the A6013. You are now back on your original route. Continue back through Bamford, turn right at the Marquis of Granby, and return to Castleton.

Drive 3

THE SOUTHERN DALES

29 miles. (47 km). Allow 1½-2 hours.

This short drive through the hills and dales on the Derbyshire/Staffordshire border will take you through a disused railway tunnel and over a ford, and these are just two of its unusual delights. There are moderate gradients and some narrow lanes to negotiate.

The charming village of Hartington in the Upper Dove Valley was granted a market charter in the early years of the thirteenth century.

From Hartington village square, take the B5054 to Warslow with the Charles Cotton Hotel on your right. Go out of the village on to the open road, crossing the River Dove at the county boundary. Ignore turnings until, after 1 mile (1.6 km), you arrive at the Hulme End village sign. Make the left turn at the Manifold Valley Hotel to Alstonefield and Wetton. After 275 metres (300 yds), take the next right to

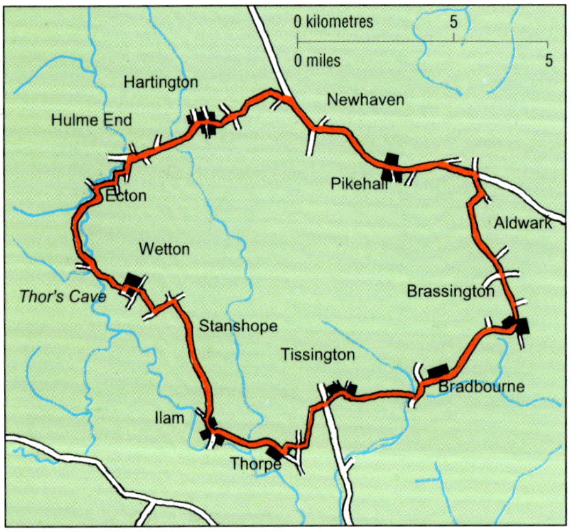

Ecton (unsigned) and run down into the valley. Ignore the left turn to Back of Ecton and continue with the River Manifold on your right.

Around the corner and ahead is the vast flank of Ecton Hill with the remains of an earlier copper mining industry scattered around. Continue along the narrow valley until you cross the river over an old bridge at Swainsley Hall. About 45 metres (50 yds) on, take a right signposted to Manifold Valley and Wetton Mill, and enter Swainsley Tunnel. The road now takes the old track bed and emerges into daylight into a delightful valley. The river is down to your left and the road takes its level course to Wetton Mill. Continue ahead, still on the old trackbed, past the 3 tons weight limit sign, to cross the river again over an old iron bridge. Look right for the elegant road bridge that crosses in parallel.

In 180 metres (200 yds), take the road that bears left, leaving the course of the old railway line at a small bridge with a no entry for vehicles sign. Climb up through trees and soon the view right opens up to reveal Thor's Cave and the valley below. After a steady climb for a mile (1.6 km) you reach Wetton. Take the left hand way into the village, signed to Alstonefield and Ilam. Passing cottages, the road bears right and you will come to a grassy triangle with the Old Royal Oak opposite. Ignore the turn to the left and continue straight ahead to Alstonefield and Ilam. Follow these signs out of the village, bearing left, and passing a playing field to the right.

A gentle descent through stone-walled fields runs down into Hopedale. Look out for a right turn up a hill signposted to Ilam and Dovedale. Continue through Stanshope, ignoring all other turnings until Ilam. From the summit with its fine views, the road runs down the valley side, into Ilam village with its Hall and Country Park on the right. Ahead is Ilam Cross. Turn left here and not ahead over the bridge. Here the River Dove runs close to the road and, coming into view left, there is the flat-topped summit of Thorpe Cloud. A left turn takes visitors to Dovedale car park but, unless you wish to stop, continue over a narrow bridge passing a farm and cattle grid. There are good views here of the entrance to Dovedale.

Go over another cattle grid and on into Thorpe. Pass through the village looking out for signs to Tissington. At the Dog and Partridge, turn right, then immediately left, to join a lane now flanked with hedges. Drive for 1 mile (1.6 km) to the crossroads with the A515. Go straight ahead through the gates into an avenue of limes, and down into Tissington.

(Above)While this spectacular yet tranquil scene is only a short walk from a car park, much of Dovedale is the preserve of walkers. (Right) Thor's Cave.

The main village street runs off to the left but continue ahead past the village pond on your right. Go out of the village past the Tissington Trail car park, over cattle grids, and on to high open pasture. Drop down through the ford, over another cattle grid and immediately join the B5056 left to Bakewell.

After 275 metres (300 yds) turn right to Bradbourne. Go through Bradbourne village and, ignoring a right turn at the telephone box, bear left to Brassington. Drive on into Brassington passing the church on your left and the Miners Arms on your right. By the pub, take the left which climbs slightly. Ignore the other minor left turns and after 90 metres (100 yds), turn left at a T-junction to Longcliffe. Climb up the hill, keeping left until the road levels out. Pass under a railway bridge and on to the crossroads ahead. Go straight across and, ignoring the turn to Aldwark on the right, continue on towards Elton and Pikehall. A twisting right and a left bring you to the A5012 crossroads. Turn left here to Newhaven in 3 miles (5 km).

At Newhaven there is a large grassy triangle at the junction with the A515. Turn right here towards Buxton. After ¾ mile (1.2 km) take the left turn to Hartington and Warslow (B5054). A final gentle descent through a pretty limestone dale brings this Drive back into Hartington village square.

Drive 4

THE WILD WEST MOORS

41 miles (66 km). Allow 3-4 hours.

Over the high western moors of the Peak National Park, this drive leaves the historic and passes through three counties to the remote and spectacular. There are moderate gradients and a variety of main and minor roads. Note: the road through the Goyt Valley is closed to traffic on Sundays and Bank Holiday Mondays, 1 May to 30 September.

This tour starts in Buxton, famous for its spa waters and its historical associations with the Dukes of Devonshire. From the Tourist Information Centre in The Crescent, head towards the Pavilion Gardens leaving the Information Centre on your right. Turn right at the Old Hall Hotel and, with the gardens and Opera House to your left, go ahead and slightly right into Water Street. On your right, pass by an old red post box. Facing you at the T-junction is the dome of the Devonshire Royal Hospital, formerly the Dukes' indoor riding school.

Turn left and bear right uphill to Whaley Bridge on the A5004. Ignore a sharp right to Leek. Passing the hospital on the right, drive up out of the town for 2 miles (3 km) on to open moorland until you reach the Peak National Park boundary sign. On the summit, take the left turn to Goyt Valley immediately passing over a cattle grid. Ahead are the moorlands above the Goyt Valley and to the right, views over Kinder Scout. After some twisting and turning, the road suddenly makes a steep, straight descent. This was the route of the long-abandoned Cromford and High Peak Railway. Cross over the dam wall to a T-junction. Go left here, marked car park, pass by the wooden barrier, and continue with Errwood Reservoir on your left. Continue on ahead noting that this is now a one-way system for several miles.

A gentle climb up the valley through groves of oak, ash, rowan, and larch brings you to a parking area beneath old quarries. Down in the valley, look for the old packhorse bridge, saved from the flooded Errwood Valley and rebuilt here. The valley narrows

The summit of Shutlingsloe, near Wildboarclough, is a well-known landmark.

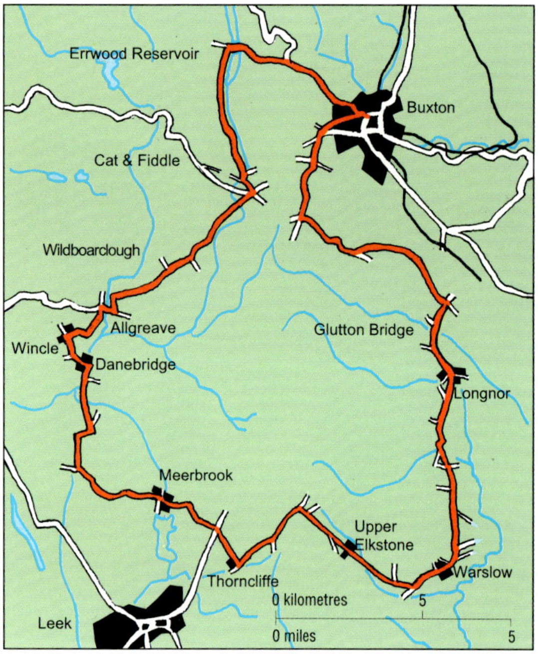

and climbs out on to open moorland. Finally the one-way section finishes at an information point and the road then turns right. After 275 metres (300 yds), take the minor turning to the left signposted to Buxton. Climb up over open moor until you reach the main Buxton to Macclesfield road at a crossroads.

Cross carefully and go ahead for 45 metres (50 yds) to a T-junction. This is the A54 Buxton to Congleton road but there are no signs here. Turn right and continue for 4½ miles (7 km) As you set off, look to the right: on the skyline is England's second highest inn, the Cat and Fiddle. Cross the county boundary into Cheshire. There is switchback ride, a summit, and then a gentle descent into the valley. Look right to Shutlingsloe summit at 506 metres (1659 ft) but ignore the right to Wildboarclough. On reaching the Rose and Crown on your left, follow the main road sharp right and down, to cross the stream over a stone bridge. In 180 metres (200 yds), take a left to Wincle and Swythamley.

Passing stone farm buildings, climb up again to a summit. The descent past Hill Top Farm brings you to a T-junction with a left to Danebridge. Drop down, keeping left passing the Ship Inn, and cross the River Dane into Staffordshire. A gentle climb above the

Dane Valley brings you to the next unsigned turn to the right beneath trees. Continue down this narrow lane past Bearda Mill, and up through a delightful glen out into open pasture. At the next T-junction, go right to Leek. Look out for the next turn to the left to Meerbrook. Another climb, this time on to rough moorland, and carry on over the summit, where there are spectacular views to the Roaches and Hen Cloud.

Drive through Meerbrook passing the Lazy Trout to the left, and cross a bridge over Tittesworth Reservoir. Continue up the lane, passing farmsteads, and there is then a final straight run to a T-junction. Turn right to Leek and, after 90 metres (100 yds), take the left to Thorncliffe. Go uphill to the hamlet and take another left at the telephone box. A steady climb up on to the moors is rewarded at the summit by fine views back over Tittesworth, the Roaches, and Ramshaw Rocks. Ignore the turn to the right and aim for the Mermaid pub 1 mile (1.6 km) ahead. Opposite the pub, take the right turn and, 275 metres (300 yds) further on, another right to Elkstone 1½ miles (2.4 km). Keep left at the fork, and a winding route takes you down into Elkstone. Go through the village, ignoring a right to Mount Pleasant Farm, and continue down the narrow lane now flanked by hedges. Pass by a left turn until the B5053 is reached at a T-junction.

Go left signposted to Longnor and, for 5½ miles (9 km), stay on this road passing through Warslow. After Warslow, avoid the right to Hartington with a similar road number and continue ahead signposted to Buxton. A long straight climb brings you to Longnor with the church ahead. At the village crossroads, go straight ahead passing the Horseshoe Inn on your left. Climb out of the village, ignoring two left turns to Hollinsclough, over the summit, and a descent to Glutton Bridge. Go over the river, back into Derbyshire and limestone country again. Follow the road, still marked 'Buxton B5053' and look ahead for Glutton Grange, a seventeenth-century farmhouse at the foot of a steep dale. Climb up past the overhanging crags until crossroads are reached. Turn left here to Dale Head.

The lane climbs up the dry dale with stone walls on either side. There are barren fields at the summit. Go over four cattle grids, past the track to Fair Thorn Farm and, a mile (1.6 km) further on, join the A53 Leek to Buxton road at Axe Edge. Turn right here and make the continuous descent into Buxton for 3 miles (5 km). Follow signs to the town centre. Pass through two sets of traffic lights and look out for the Pavilion and Opera House on your right. Take the right by the Opera House and return to your starting point.

(Above) The Upper Goyt Valley was flooded to form Errwood Reservoir, one of two supplying water to Stockport. (Below) Close to the drive is Three Shires Head where Derbyshire, Staffordshire, and Cheshire meet.

THE PEAK DISTRICT

The diversity and beauty of scenery in the Peak District National Park make it one of the most popular National Parks in the world, appealing to walkers, climbers, and potholers, as well as to cyclists and motorists. The Millstone Grit and limestone rocks bestow a unique character to the region, from desolate moorlands, peaks and tors, to lush dales and deep caverns.

Illustrated Walks and Drives in the Peak District is an invaluable guide to the traveller wishing to explore the area, whether it be to participate in the pre-Christian rite of well-dressing, or to walk the Pennine Way route leading to the top of Kinder Scout. To take a stroll along the Cromford canal offers the visitor a glimpse into the village's industrial past, where Sir Richard Arkwright operated the first water-powered cotton mill. There are opportunities to visit the magnificent, seventeenth-century Chatsworth House, home to the Dukes of Devonshire, as well as Eyam, the village decimated by plague in the mid-1600s.

This guide is part of Pitkin's Illustrated Walks and Drives series, which also includes the Cotswolds, the Lake District, the North York Moors, Snowdonia, and the Yorkshire Dales.

Edited, designed, and produced by Curtis Garratt Limited, Horton cum Studley, Oxford OX9 1BT

Text and all photographs by Mike Williams

Printed in Great Britain by Cedar Colour Ltd., Chandlers Ford, Hants.

ISBN 0 85372 549 7 192/15

PITKIN

ISBN 0-85372-549-7